**Fred Edrissi**

# Chef's Healthy
# Desserts

## Satisfy your sweet tooth with healthy ingredients and natural sweeteners

# Contents

## Chef's Healthy Desserts

## Dessert Recipes

Note: Conversions in this book (from imperial to metric) are not exact. They have been rounded to the nearest measurement for convenience. Exact measurements are given in imperial. The recipes in this book are by no means to be taken as therapeutic. They simply promote the philosophy of both the author and *alive* books in relation to whole foods, health and nutrition, while incorporating the practical advice given by the author in the first section of the book.

# Chef's Healthy Desserts

As long as your ingredients are natural and wholesome desserts can be both satisfying and nutritious.

## The Sweet Temptation · · · · · · · · · · · · · · ·

Ahhh, the delectable dessert. Many of us have a sweet tooth to some degree and consider our indulgences into desserts to be sinful. However, there are many ways to enjoy delicious, "to-die-for" desserts, without the guilt; and without the unhealthy white sugar and other ingredients that are often the sources of our guilt.

I am not a big sweet eater myself, however, my wife is—she loves sweets! (I think she would prefer if I were a pastry chef.) But she doesn't like just any kind of sweets. They must be specially made—nice, light and delicious. I am forever coming up with new ways to delight her sweet tooth, without rotting it. I want to keep her healthy and because the white refined sugar that most recipes call for is not healthy, I use substitutes. Natural sweeteners such as natural sugar cane crystals, maple syrup and honey are much healthier choices. Whole grain flours, such as whole wheat and kamut, add nutrition to desserts instead of the empty calories that white refined flour provides.

I truly enjoy the challenge of creating healthy desserts and am pleased to share my discoveries and secrets with you. Desserts don't have to be sinful any longer!

## The Value of Sweetness · · · · · · · · · · · · · · ·

Sugar wasn't always sinful, in fact, it was once quite valuable. It is said that a Greek expedition in 325 BC discovered "sweet large grass" in Persia. This sweet-tasting grass was simply chewed and eaten on its own. The thicker and older stems were pressed to extract the juice and this juice then was dried to form crystals quite similar to the modern refined sugar. This was the beginning of a very large and profitable business.

By the 18th century, sugar was a precious spice. Because of its high value it was found only in wealthy households. It was locked up in special boxes, just like gold and jewelry. To the Chinese, sugar was so valuable that they traded it for silk and jade stones. The Dutch, the British, the French and the Asians—everybody was in the sugar business.

### That was Then—This is Now
Today, sugar is valuable in a very different way. The

processed, white refined sugar, devoid of any nutritional value for the body, is added to just about every packaged and canned food imaginable to increase the palatability of processed foods. Therefore, it is valuable to so-called food manufacturers, but is of no value to the body as it is not good for consumption in any way.

White sugar is found not only in sweet baked goods and desserts but also in ready-made foods such as cereals, soups and frozen foods, and even in canned vegetables. Read the labels of the so-called foods people buy and see for yourself.

White, refined sugar is the result of a complicated industrial procedure. After various chemical treatments, sugar cane and sugar beet are turned not into the carefully made crystals of the days gone by, but are quickly and economically made into a cheap white crystallized product that is totally denatured and is able to sit on the supermarket shelf for years.

## Sugar Addiction . . . . . . . . . . . . . . . . . . . . .

White sugar is undoubtedly the most overlooked drug on the market. Yes, I said drug. It does, after all, have side effects and is addictive—the more you eat it the more you want it and the more your body gets used to getting it.

*The addiction to sugar usually begins as a small child.*

While my wife did not develop her sweet tooth until she was an adult (she used to eat raw vegetables, including garlic, for treats when she was young), the addiction to sugar usually begins as a small child. Baby cookies and crackers, and children's juices and lunch snacks all contain sugar. Children's taste buds get used to it and sugar becomes a normal part of the diet. Today the annual consumption of sugar per person in North America is 40 kilograms (88 pounds)! No wonder every fourth school child is overweight.

This unnatural dietary habit weakens the immune system and results in illness and overall poor health. Once sugar is cut out of the diet, cravings will not occur and sugar will taste unnaturally sweet to the taste buds.

### The Side Effects of White Sugar

White sugar supplies the body with calories without nutritional benefits. So when the body is required to metabolize this empty food it robs the body of stored vitamins and minerals in order to

do so. Therefore eating sugar leads to malnutrition and has also been linked with numerous conditions such as obesity, cancer and diabetes, to name only a few.

People say they eat sugar for an "energy rush" or a "boost." True, sugar will give you a boost, but this boost is only temporary; when it's over, your energy level will be lower than before you ate the sugary treat.

## Alternatives to White Sugar . . . . . . . . . . . .

There are some wonderful alternatives to white sugar. However, please remember that sugar is sugar, good or bad, and should not be eaten in large quantities. Just because the following options are natural, that does not mean you should fill yourselves with them. Diabetics, especially, need to watch their intake of sugar even when it is from a natural source like fruit.

### Natural Sugar

**Natural sugar crystals may be equally substituted for white sugar in your recipes.**

There are many types of natural sugar crystals on the market. Some are superior to others simply because of the way they're made. No matter what type you buy, be sure that it is made from organically grown sugar cane. I usually buy one of the two products described below.

Sucanat: This is a natural sweetener with a higher nutritional value than white sugar, and a natural rich flavor. Its consistency (it's available in both powder and granule form) is perfect for creating desserts-even baked goods. It is instantly soluble and can replace the white sugar recipes call for with an convenient 1:1 ratio. Unlike the process used to make white refined sugar, the process used to make Sucanat preserves the natural taste and nutrition, without preservatives or additives, and actually has a lower level of sucrose than refined sugar.

Fresh sugar cane stalks are pressed to release their juices. This juice is then dehydrated through a crystallization process, which is when the round, porous Sucanat granules are formed. Sucanat has an unlimited shelf life when stored at 70 to 80° Fahrenheit (21 to 27° Celsius).

Rapadura: This natural sugar is also an excellent product and used by some of the best chefs, and in some of the finest bakeries, in the world. While most of the other natural sugar producers separate the molasses from the sugar at some stage during production, Rapadura does not. This results in a good nutritional profile, which includes a significant mineral and vitamin content.

## The Honey Bee's Natural Sweetener

Our ancestors learned about honey, and its wonderful taste, about 15,000 years ago. Since then it has earned a valuable reputation throughout the world and the ages. Even the Bible mentions "the land where milk and honey flow."

The sugar in honey has been predigested by bees and reduced to fructose and dextrose (simple sugars), making it easy for us to digest. In addition, raw honey contains modest amounts of many vitamins, minerals and enzymes. Its moisture-absorbing properties make it a good antibacterial agent, as bacteria need moisture to thrive. Harmful germs, for instance, die within forty-eight hours when introduced into pure honey, which is why fresh honey has traditionally been used to dress wounds.

Heating honey over 38° Celsius (100° Fahrenheit) will kill its nutrients. So, adding honey to your tea will sweeten it, but won't be of any nutritional value. Buy unfiltered, unheated, unprocessed honey and store it in a dry dark place protected from the air and humidity. It is an excellent alternative to sugar for your desserts.

**Replace 2 tablespoons of white sugar with 1 tablespoon of honey, in your recipes.**

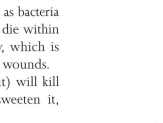

**Maple syrup is sweeter than sugar. Replace 100 grams (3.5 ounces) of sugar with 75 milliliters (2.5 ounces) of syrup. If baking with it, consider the fluid adjustment: Reduce 2 tablespoons of another other liquid when using 75 milliliters of syrup.**

Because of its high sugar content, honey is not appropriate for people with diabetes. Honey should never be fed to an infant under one year of age because, in its natural form, it can contain spores of the bacteria that cause botulism. It is not a problem for adults or children over one, who have a more developed digestive tract that won't allow the toxin to colonize and cause disease.

## Maple Syrup

It's an honor for me to discuss maple syrup in this book, while living and working in beautiful Canada–the country that discovered and produces this tasty treat.

Long before the first white settlers came to North America, the indigenous people already knew how to collect the sap from maple trees and make it into maple syrup each spring season. They were willing to give their knowledge to the white people in the early days of colonization. They showed the French settlers how to tap the trunks, harvest the sap and boil it to evaporate part of the water until syrup was left. The procedure has developed somewhat, however, maple syrup still begins with tree tapping and is still as natural and sweet as it was over a century ago.

| Nutritional Value of Maple Syrup (per 100 grams) | |
|---|---|
| Carbohydrates | 66 g |
| Saccharide | 59-69 g |
| Fructose and glucose | 1.4-1.8 g |
| Sodium | 0.1-2.5 mg |
| **Minerals:** | |
| Potassium | 150-200 mg |
| Calcium | 40-100 mg |
| Magnesium | 10-30 mg |
| Phosphorus | 5-12.5 mg |
| Iron | 0.1-1.5 mg |
| **Vitamins:** | |
| $B^2$ (Riboflavin) | 0.006 mg |
| $B^3$ (Niacin) | 0.3 mg |
| $B^5$ (Pantothenic acid) | 0.6 mg |

## The Truth About White Flour ··········

Refined white flour has been denatured and bleached and, as a result, has about as much nutritional value as cardboard. The grain is "cleansed" of all perishable components that will deteriorate and hinder machine processing. The vitamin- and mineral-rich parts of the kernel, the oil-rich germ and the valuable bran are separated during this process and are used for cattle feed! Whole grain loses 10 to 100 percent of its vitamin, mineral and fiber content during the commercial milling and refining process.

> All flour is made from grain, however, they are not all whole grain flours! All-purpose white flour is stripped of much of its composition. The end product is an excellent source of gluten (that's why it still works when baking) but it is definitely no longer a whole grain and no longer nutritious.

People are so used to buying white flour and eating white bread and baked desserts that they actually believe it is wholesome and natural, however, that couldn't be farther from the truth.

### The Side Effects of White Flour

White, refined flour has a higher ratio of gluten, which, when ingested, has been shown to inhibit peristalsis of the intestinal tract, resulting in chronic constipation. The general public may not consider themselves constipated unless they go weeks without a bowel movement. The reality is that those who eat a whole foods diet with true nutrients have a bowel movement after each meal.

White flour lacks fiber, and eating inadequate amounts of fiber may lead to constipation, diabetes, obesity, arteririscleroses, gallbladder problems, skin disease and colon cancer. Fiber is necessary as it transports the bad cholesterol out of the body. The B-vitamin group, which is responsible for a well-functioning metabolism among many

*Whole grains have a superior nutritional value compared to white flour.*

things, is lost during the refining process. If we look at the nutrients lost during the processing of white refined flour, we can see the exact nutrients that are lacking in our daily nutrition. That's why it's such a wonderful opportunity to make your own desserts and take advantage of the nutrients available in healthful ingredients. That's why it's important to choose whole grain products for your tasty creations.

## Why are Whole Grain Products Healthier? . . .

Whole grains offer a variety of nutrients. All grains are high in natural carbohydrates that easily convert into energy. (They do not cause high cholesterol). Foods prepared with whole grains have a superior nutritional value containing high amounts of proteins, fiber (roughage), vitamins and minerals. Since these precious nutrients are concentrated in the outer membrane and the germ of the grain, it is important to eat the whole grain for better nutrition. Whole grains are not fattening, just more filling because of their nutritional value and fiber content.

Whole grains contain a high amount of insoluble fiber, which keeps the intestinal flora healthy and increases stool volume considerably. This is very importance for health, because the increased volume of the stool speeds up the elimination process, decreasing

the time it takes to get through the intestinal tract, which decreases the risk for chronic intestinal diseases, including cancer.

Desserts prepared with natural organic whole grain flour might be more costly, but in the long run it will save medical costs associated with degenerative diseases such as arthritis, cancer, diabetes, heart problems and many others.

## Favorite Whole Grains for Dessert Baking

**Whole wheat:** This popular grain makes up more than 75 percent of our grain consumpion, in the form of breads, pasta, cereal, etc. It is great for desserts too! Whole wheat flour contains as much gluten as white flour, plus all the added nutritional value.

**Corn:** This yellow flour is best when stone ground from the whole kernel. Corn contains cancer-fighting agents as well as valuable vitamins and minerals.

**Kamut:** This whole grain is usually well-tolerated by wheat-sensitive people although its gluten content is low so it is often combined with a bit of wheat flour.

**Oats:** Wonderful for desserts, this flour adds a sweet flavor of its own. It is also known to help lower cholesterol, is high in protein and is a good source of vitamin E.

**Spelt:** An ancient variety of wheat, originating in Mesopotamia and Persia, spelt was used by the Greeks and Romans. The baking properties of spelt are similar to those of wheat and can therefore be used in place of it for those with a wheat allergy or simply for variety. It is one of the easiest grains to digest and is high in B vitamins.

## Let's Have Dessert! . . . . . . . . . . . . . . . . . .

As you can see, desserts can be delicious without being sinful. As long as your ingredients are natural and wholesome (and you don't overdo it on the sweets) there is no reason to be deprived of treats or nutrition. The next section of the book will introduce you to a wide variety of wholesome ingredients that, with some creativity and a love for desserts, will be both satisfying and nutritious. Enjoy!

# Dessert Recipes

Enjoy delicious desserts, without guilt, by using wholesome ingredients and natural sweeteners as your ingredients.

# Apple Fritters

2 large, firm organic apples, peeled, cored and cut in ½" slices

1 tbsp dried cane sugar

¼ cup (100g) dried cane sugar powder

1 tsp lemon juice

1 cup (440g) whole wheat flour

2 free-range eggs, separated

2-3 tbsp good cognac (or apple cider)

⅔ cup (180ml) natural milk or water

Pinch salt

1 tbsp cold-pressed almond oil

⅔ cup (150ml) coconut butter

1 tbsp cinnamon (mixed with 3 tbsp dried cane sugar)

Sprinkle dried cane sugar and lemon juice over the apple slices. Cover the apples and set aside. Sift the flour into a bowl, add egg yolks, cognac, milk, salt, almond oil, ¼ cup of cane sugar powder and mix into a runny dough. Whisk egg white until stiff and fold under the dough.

In a cast iron skillet heat the coconut butter. Dip the apple slices into the dough, making sure that they are completely coated. Fry apples on both sides until golden brown. Coat in cinnamon/sugar mixture. Serve warm.

Serves 4

apple

For even better results, slightly coat the apples with whole wheat flour before dipping them into the dough.

# Apple Pancake

A variation on the traditional, personal pancake, this large pancake is healthy, delicious and adds a different flair to the concept. It may be served for breakfast, lunch or for high tea.

## Batter:

½ **cup (220g) whole wheat flour**

**2 free-range eggs**

**Pinch salt**

**Pinch nutmeg**

**Pinch cinnamon**

½ **cup (120ml) milk**

**1 tbsp cinnamon for garnish**

**1 tbsp butter**

**2 tbsp honey**

**1 tbsp butter** (to sauté apples)

## Apple Slices:

**1 large organic apple**

**2 tbsp dried cane sugar**

**1 tbsp cinnamon for garnish**

This type of pancake is like one large pancake that is cut in pie-like slices for serving. In a large mixing bowl combine all ingredients for the pancake batter and mix thoroughly. Peel and core the apple and slice it into round ½" discs. In a pan (one that can be put in the oven later) sauté both sides of the apple slices with butter.

Pour batter mixture over the apple slices. Cook for 4 to 5 minutes on medium heat to brown the bottom of the pancake. To brown the top of the pancake, put the pan in the preheated oven at 280° F (140°C). Bake for 5 minutes or until brown. Portion the pancake and serve.

Serves 2 to 4

*apple*

# Poached Apple and Pear with Custard

With a little time and patience this beautiful dessert is a delight to both create and eat. The fruit and almonds make it a nutritious and filling treat as well.

**1 baking pan** (8")

**1 round pastry cake**
(page 26)

**2 organic apples**

**1 organic pear**

**1 cup** (240ml) **red wine**

**2 tbsp maple syrup**

**1 cinnamon stick**

**1 star anise**

½ **whole nutmeg**
(or ½ tsp powder)

**1 tbsp natural,
organic butter**

¼ **cup** (80g)
**sliced almonds**

### Custard:

**2 cups** (480ml) **natural
whipping cream**

**4 tbsp dried cane sugar**

**3 free-range egg yolks**

**Seeds from 1 vanilla bean**
(or 1 tbsp natural
vanilla extract)

Peel and core apples and pear from the bottom, leaving them whole and with the stem intact. Combine red wine, maple syrup, cinnamon, star anise and nutmet in a pot. Bring to a boil, immediately lower heat and place apples and pear in mixture. Poach for 7 to 10 minutes on low heat. Grease the inside of the cake form with butter and place the pastry cake in the form. Sprinkle roasted almonds on the pastry. Remove the poached fruit from pot and cut each in half. Cut slits in the backs of the apple and pear halves and set aside.

To make the custard, combine whipping cream, dried cane sugar, egg yolks and vanilla seeds. Stir with a wooden spoon on medium heat until thick. Place apple and pear halves (slit sides up) in the cake form and pour custard over top. Bake in preheated oven at 325° F (163°C) for 20 minutes, or until the custard begins to brown.

Serve warm.

Serves 4

pear

# Apple Pear Strudel

While this recipe takes a bit of time and effort, it is well worth it. It is an Austrian specialty, which is especially popular around Christmas time. Serve it warm with vanilla ice cream. You will love it!

## Strudel Dough:

1 cup (440g) **whole wheat flour** (double sifted)

1 **free-range egg**

**Pinch sea salt**

2 tsp **coconut oil**

½ cup (220g) **butter, room temperature**

4 tbsp **cold natural milk or water**

**extra flour to roll dough**

1 **free-range egg, beaten**

## Filling:

3 **organic apples, peeled, cored and thinly sliced**

2 **organic pears, peeled, cored and thinly sliced**

¼ cup (100g) **raisins**

3 tbsp **rum or apple juice**

¼ cup (100g) **sour cream or kefir**

2 tsp **cinnamon powder**

½ cup (160g) **almonds**

½ cup (200g) **dried cane sugar**

Pour sifted flour onto a clean counter top and form an indent in the middle of the pile. Add egg, salt and oil to the indentation. Add 1 tablespoon of the butter and start kneading into a dough. Slowly add milk and continue kneading until dough becomes elastic. Put the dough in the fridge for 1 hour. While the dough is in the fridge, peel core and thinly slice the apples and pears for the filling. Put the raisins from the filling ingredients in the rum to soak for 1 hour.

Take the dough out of the fridge and let it sit for 20 minutes. Dust countertop with a bit of flour and roll out the dough, as thin as possible, into a square shape. Lay a kitchen towel flat on the counter and dust with flour. Place the dough on the towel. Melt the rest of the butter and brush the dough with it (put extra butter aside to use later). Arrange apple and pear slices on the dough. With the back of a spoon, spread the sour cream over top. Sprinkle the rest of the ingredients, including the rum-soaked raisins, evenly over top.

With the help of the towel, roll dough up tightly like a jelly roll. Grease a baking sheet with some of the melted butter and brush the rest of the butter onto the strudel. Put the strudel in the oven and bake for 20 minutes at 380° F (195° C), or until golden. Take strudel out of the oven and brush it with the beaten egg. Return to oven and bake for another 10 minutes.

Serves 6

# Apricot Squares

The apricot is a tasty package of nutrition, with cancer-fighting properties. This recipe offers something for both your health and your sweet tooth.

**2 pieces cake pastry, cut into squares** (page 26)

½ **cup** (150g) **dried apricots, marinated**

½ **cup** (200g) **Mascarpone cheese** (Italian cream cheese)

I tbsp **macadamia nuts, chopped**

¼ **cup** (60ml) **natural whipping cream**

I tbsp **cocoa powder** (eg. Rapunzel cocoa powder)

**Apricot Marinade:**

2 tbsp **luke warm water**

I tbsp **maple syrup**

I tbsp **apricot liqueur**

In a large mixing bowl combine the apricot marinade ingredients and marinade apricots for 2 hours. Remove apricots and set aside. In another bowl combine Mascarpone cheese, nuts, whipping cream and 2 tablespoons of the left over marinade, and mix thoroughly, until smooth. Spread one layer of cheese mixture over the pastry and top with marinated apricots. Repeat and put second cake pastry on top. Spread the remaining cream cheese mixture on top and dust it with cocoa powder.

Serves 6

apricot

For a fancy presentation, place star anise on the squares and serving plates before dusting with powder. Then remove the star anise to show powdery stars.

# Raspberry Mascarpone Rolls

## Pastry Cake:

**4 free-range egg whites**

**Pinch sea salt**

¼ **cup (80g) natural honey**

**4 free-range egg yolks**

⅔ **cup (100g) millet or Kamut flour**

**1 tsp natural vanilla extract**

**Rind from** ½ **lemon**

**2 tbsp melted butter**

## Filling:

**1 cup (400g) Mascarpone cheese** (or natural cream cheese)

½ **cup (125g) raspberry or blackberry coulis** (page 50)

**2 tbsp maple syrup**

**1 tsp natural vanilla extract**

**Dash raspberry liqueur** (optional)

## Glaze:

**2 tbsp apricot marmalade** (page 28)

**2 tbsp water**

½ **cup (125g) pistachio nuts, grated**

Pastry Cake: Preheat oven to 380° F (200°C). Whisk egg whites together with salt until stiff. Slowly add honey, in small amounts, while continually whisking until the mixture becomes shiny. Add egg yolk while whisking and continue until mixture turns slightly yellow and creamy. Finely grind millet, using a coffee grinder or food processor, and fold under mixture with a spatula. Add vanilla extract and lemon zest. Grease baking sheet with butter, put parchment paper on baking sheet and grease parchment paper. Pour dough onto the sheet and spread it evenly. Bake for approximately 10 minutes. Take out and set aside.

Filling: For the filling, mix all ingredients together and spread on the pastry sheet. Roll pastry sheet carefully (like a jelly roll) using the parchment paper and gradually peeling it away, while rolling.

Glaze: Mix apricot jam and water, and brush the pastry with this mixture. Sprinkle with pistachio nuts.

Serves 4 to 8

# California Fruit Cake

10-12" rectangle pastry cake (page 26)

1 brick natural cream cheese

1 ½ tsp honey

2 tsp natural vanilla extract

¼ cup (100g) apricot marmalade (recipe below)

¼ cup (100g) strawberries, sliced

1 large kiwi, sliced

½ ripe papaya, sliced

1 large orange, cut in segments

1 tbsp pistachio nuts, grated

Mix cream cheese, honey and vanilla extract. Spread over the pastry dough and arrange all fruit on top of the spread. In a small bowl, mix apricot marmalade and orange juice and brush this mixture over the fruit until shiny.

# Apricot Marmalade

4 lbs (1.8 kilo) fresh apricots, peeled and pitted

2 cups (750 g) dried cane sugar

2 tbsp lemon juice

2 tbsp (60 g) agar agar (natural gelatine thickener)

3 tbsp of rum, apricot liqueur or Grand Marnier (optional)

If fresh apricots are not in season, use ½ pound of dried apricots and soak them for 2 hours before following the rest of the recipe instructions.

Put half of the apricots in a blender and blend until smooth. Finely chop the other half of the apricots. Put all ingredients (except for the alcohol) into a pot and bring to a boil, stirring the entire time. Let boil for half a minute (still stirring) then turn the heat down to medium. Continue to stir for 5 more minutes or until the mixture thickens to desired consistency. If the marmalade isn't thick enough, add more agar agar. If it gets too thick, add a bit of orange juice or water. Once desired consistency develops, remove from heat and stir in alcohol.

Put in sterile, hot jars (leaving ½" of space at the top) and refrigerate or keep in a cool spot.

Makes 4 medium size jars

# Cajun Bread Pudding

I loaf whole wheat bread, sliced

I tbsp organic butter

I large ripe banana, sliced ¼" thick

I large organic apple, peeled and thinly sliced

I tbsp cinnamon

Pinch nutmeg

Pinch cloves

I tbsp dried cane sugar

¼ cup (100g) raisins

3 tbsp rum (or water)

½ cup natural whipping cream

½ cup pecan nuts

½ cup organic butter

Soak raisins in the rum for 1 hour. Grease a medium size casserole dish with one tablespoon of butter. Place bread slices in the casserole dish. Spread banana over bread and add apple and all spices including dried cane sugar. Add rum-soaked raisins and top with whipping cream. Add pecan pieces and save a few for garnish. Melt butter and pour over top. Bake in preheated oven at 380° F (200° C) for 20 to 25 minutes and serve warm.

Serve with ice cream or fresh fruit preserve (page 52).

Serves 4

banana

# Kiwi and Pear Sorbet

Exotic, light and nutritious, this recipe is an easy route to sorbet heaven.

### Kiwi Sorbet:

**4 ripe kiwis, peeled and cut in chunks**

**2 tbsp honey**

¼ **cup (60ml) organic apple juice**

**1 free-range egg white**

Using a blender, combine kiwis with honey and apple juice until smooth. Freeze for at least one hour, or until it is slushy. In a large bowl, whisk egg white until stiff. Fold semi-frozen kiwi mixture into the egg white and combine thoroughly. Freeze again until firm (about 4 to 5 hours). Serve sorbet balls in glasses for a special touch.

### Pear Sorbet:

**2 ripe pears, peeled and cut in chunks**

**2 tbsp of honey**

**1 tsp lemon juice**

¼ **cup (60ml) organic pear juice**

**1 free-range egg white**

Follow same directions as above, substituting pear for kiwi.

Serves 2

pear

kiwi

# Mousse au Chocolate

No chocolate-lover can resist the traditional mousse. This healthy version is truly "to die for."

1 cup (240g) **unsweetened bitter chocolate**

3 **free-range egg yolks**

¼ **cup** (100g) **dried cane sugar**

1 **tsp natural vanilla extract**

3 oz (85 g) **cocoa**

3 **free-range egg whites** (beat separately)

3 **tbsp dried cane sugar powder**

½ **cup** (120ml) **natural whipping cream**

Melt chocolate in a double bath. Make sure that the chocolate is tempered and not hot. In the meantime beat the egg yolks, dried cane sugar and vanilla extract until smooth and shiny. Add cocoa powder and melted chocolate.

In a second bowl beat the egg white with the dried cane sugar powder until stiff. First, fold whipping cream into the chocolate mixture with a spatula. Then, very carefully, fold the egg white under the mixture. Pour mixture in serving dish or glasses and refrigerate for 3 to 4 hours before serving.

Serves 2

*free-range eggs*

## Making a Double Bath

Fill a pot half full with water and put on medium heat. Fit a mixing bowl on top of the pot. Place the chocolate in the bowl. The steam from the water will warm the bowl, which will melt the chocolate without subjecting it to direct heat.

# Country Berry Pie

### Pastry:

**1 cup (440g) whole wheat flour**

**Pinch salt**

**1 free-range egg yolk**

**4 tbsp natural butter** (room temperature)

**2 tbsp cold natural milk or water**

**⅛ cup (50g) dried cane sugar**

**¼ cup (100g) grated hazelnuts, for garnish**

**⅛ cup (50g) dried cane sugar, for garnish**

**1 tsp cinnamon**

### Berry Filling:

**2 ½ cups (450g) each of mixed berries, strawberries, blackberries, raspberries, blueberries, and cherries**

**1 large organic apple**

**1 large organic pear**

**1 tsp nutmeg**

**½ tsp cloves**

**1 tbsp unpasteurized honey**

**Rind of 1 orange and 1 lime, grated**

**½ cup natural whipping cream, for garnish**

Sift flour onto counter top and sprinkle with salt. Make a 1" dent in the flour pile and add egg yolk and 2 tablespoons of butter. Mix egg and butter into the flour with your hands (dough should be crumbly). Add your milk or water and mix again until dense (dough should be smooth now). Put the dough in plastic wrap and set in the fridge for a minimum of 1 hour, but preferably 3 hours. (This step will give you a crispier piecrust later on.)

Remove from fridge and let sit for 20 minutes, or until room temperature. Add 2 tablespoons of butter and knead again. Dust your countertop with flour and roll out the dough with a rolling pin. Because we want the dough to be round (about ½" thick) continually turn the dough when rolling. The width of the dough should be about 14" across for an 8" pie plate. Place the dough in the pie plate, making sure that it overlaps the pan by at least 3" all around. With a fork, prick the dough on the bottom of the pie plate several times so the pastry doesn't bubble when baking.

Combine all filling ingredients and add to the pastry. Fold the overhanging pastry onto filling (leaving the center uncovered). Bake the pie on a rack in middle of the oven for 45 minutes at 350° F (180°C). Directly after removing the pie from the oven, sprinkle hazelnuts, sugar and cinnamon on top.

# Cardamom Crème Brûlée

Cardamom is an oriental spice with a very distinct flowery taste.

**1 qt (1 L) natural cream**

**½ cup (125g) dried cane sugar**

**4 free-range egg yolks**

**5 pieces cardamom**

**Juice from 1 orange**

**Zest from 1 orange**

**1 ½ tbsp dried cane sugar, for garnish**

Put all ingredients in a saucepan and stir until the mixture develops a syrup-like consistency. Strain the mixture through a sieve and pour into individual soufflé dishes. Set the dishes in a lasagna-type pan and carefully pour water around the dishes, until about ⅔ of the height of the dishes are under water.

Bake at 280° F (145° C) for 45 minutes. Set aside until cool to room temperature and refrigerate for at least 1 hour before serving. Remove from fridge and sprinkle dried cane sugar over top. Put dishes on top shelf in the oven under the broiler for 1 to 2 minutes, or until sugar caramelizes. Remove immediately and serve.

Serves 4

*orange*

# Fruit Cup

This recipe is simple to make, yet elegant enough to serve to the fussiest guests. Dinner guests aside, this is a fun way to eat a serving of fresh fruit.

**2 large crêpes** (page 42)

**Cream Cheese Filling:**

**1 tbsp dried cane sugar**

½ **cup (200g) natural cream cheese or kefir**

**1 tbsp lemon juice**

**2 tbsp maple syrup**

**2 tbsp Cointreau**
(or orange juice concentrate)

**Fruit Filling:**

½ **cup (120g) mango, cut in ½" chunks**

½ **cup (120g) papaya, cut in ½" chunks**

½ **cup (120g) strawberries, halved**

**1 organic apple, cut in ½" chunks**

**1 orange, cut in segments**

**2 tbsp grated hazelnuts**

Place the crêpes in muffin forms or soufflé dishes. Blind bake the crêpes to make cups, by putting a ball of tin foil in the center of each crêpe (a handful of dried beans works, too). Bake for 4 to 5 minutes at 320° F (160°C) until the crêpes are firm and they look like small cups. In a medium bowl mix all fruit ingredients together. In another bowl, mix all of the cream cheese filling ingredients together.

Put 1 tablespoon of cream cheese filling in the bottom of each cup and fill the rest of the cup with the fruit mixture. Then put 1 tablespoon of the cream cheese filling on top of each fruit cup and sprinkle hazelnuts over top.

Serves 2

mango

strawberry

# Crêpe Suzettes

To enjoy one of Europe's oldest dishes, simply call your pancakes by their French name: crêpes. There are endless ways to prepare crêpes. Crêpe Suzettes is just one variation. You can also try your crêpes with raspberries, blackberries or any number of fruits.

## Crêpes:

½ **cup** (100g) **whole wheat flour**

½ **cup** (120ml) **water**

½ **cup** (120ml) **natural milk** (or apple cider)

**Pinch nutmeg**

**Pinch of salt**

**2 free-range eggs**

**1 tbsp organic butter**

## Sauce:

**Juice from 1 orange**

**2 tbsp honey**

**2 tbsp butter**

**2 oz Grand Marnier** (or any type of orange liquor)

**Rind from one orange**

**2 oranges, cut into segments**

In a large mixing bowl combine flour, water and milk or apple cider, nutmeg and salt. Mix thoroughly. Add eggs and stir until a smooth batter forms. Let batter rest in the fridge for half an hour.

Add about ¼ teaspoon of butter to a small non-stick pan (preferrably 8 "/15 cm in diameter), and melt at medium heat. Cover the bottom of the pan with the melted butter. Add 4 tablespoons (60 ml) of batter to the pan. There should be just enough to cover the bottom of the pan by lifting and tilting it to spread the batter around. After 2 minutes or so the pancake should form a bubble. This is the precise moment to flip it over and fry the other side for another 2 to 3 minutes. Continue this procedure until you use all the batter. Set the crêpes aside.

In another sauté pan heat up orange juice, honey, 1 tablespoon of butter and Grand Marnier for 2 to 3 minutes. Fold the crêpes in half and then in half again, and lay them in the pan with the honey mixture. Heat both sides for 1 minute each. You can either add orange segments and orange rind and serve in the pan (the way they do in France), or remove the crêpes from the pan, put on serving plates, top with orange and pour honey mixture over top.

Serves 4

# Floating Islands in Caramel

Light and sweet, this dessert is fun to make and even more fun to serve and eat.

## Vanilla Sauce:

**1 qt (1 L) natural milk**

**1 ½ tbsp honey**

**4 free-range egg yolks**

**⅛ cup (30ml) natural cream**

**Seeds from 2 vanilla beans or 2 tbsp natural vanilla extract**

## Caramel Topping:

**1 tbsp water**

**3½ tbsp dried cane sugar**

**⅛ cup (30ml) natural cream**

## Floating Islands:

**4 free-range egg whites**

**2 tbsp of dried cane sugar powder**

**¼ cup (100g) whole pistachio nuts, shelled**

**¼ cup (60ml) natural cream**

Vanilla Sauce: Heat the milk in a saucepan. Add honey, egg yolks, cream and vanilla seeds. Stir with a wooden spoon until it has a syrup-like consistency. Strain through a sieve.

Caramel Topping: In a separate pot put 1 tablespoon of water and 3 ½ tablespoons of dried cane sugar and melt it. Add the rest of the cream and reduce until thick and caramel colored.

Floating Islands: Whisk the egg whites with 2 tablespoons of dried cane sugar powder until stiff.

Fill a large frying pan ⅔ full of water and put on medium heat. Shortly before water starts boiling, portion the egg white into 4 portions with a tablespoon and place in hot water until they are firm.

Pour the Vanilla Sauce into deep dishes and place 2 floating islands (egg whites) in each bowl. Drizzle Caramel Sauce on top and garnish with pistachio nuts.

Serves 2

# Red Wine Poached Pear

This elegant dessert looks complicated (and is therefore impressive to serve), however, it is simple to make. Take your time and enjoy creating this wonderful and healthy dessert.

**1 large organic pear**

½ **cup** (120ml) **Grenadine** (pomegranate syrup)

**1 cup** (240ml) **red wine**

**1 cinnamon stick**

**2 cloves**

**1 tbsp honey**

**1 pastry cake** (½" thick, 4" diameter) (page 36)

¼ **cup** (100g) **Mascarpone** (Italian cream cheese)

**2 tbsp blackberry or apricot marmalade** (page 28)

Peel and core the pear from the bottom, leaving the top (with the stem) intact. In a pot, combine the Grenadine, red wine, cinnamon, cloves and honey and bring to a boil. As soon as it boils, turn heat to low and set pear in the pot. Poach, uncovered, for 10 minutes.

In the meantime cut the pastry to dimensions specified. Mix Mascarpone and blackberry marmalade and spread on top of the cake pastry. Remove poached pear and slice it, from the bottom, up to within 1" of the top so that when it has been sliced all the way around you can fan it out over top of the pastry and cheese.

Serves 1

blackberry

pear

# Coffee Cream with Coconut

1 ⅔ cups (400ml) **milk**

3 **free-range eggs**

2 **free-range egg yolks**

¼ **cup** (80g) **dried cane sugar**

¼ **cup** (100ml) **strong instant coffee**

1 tbsp **coconut, shredded**

### For garnish:

¼ **cup** (100ml) **whipping cream**

½ tbsp **powder dried cane sugar**

1 tbsp **cocoa powder**

In a medium pot bring milk to a boil. Turn off the stove but keep the milk on the burner to stay warm. Preheat the oven to 300° F (150° C). Beat the whole eggs and egg yolks with the dried cane sugar until the mixture looks like a pale, foamy cream. Slowly add the instant coffee while continuing to stir. Slowly pour the milk into the mixture and then add shredded coconut, continuing to stir the entire time. Pour the cream mixture into small soufflé dishes. If you don't have soufflé dishes you can use coffee cups.

Set the dishes in a lasagna-type pan and carefully pour water around the dishes, until it covers about ⅔ of the height of the dishes. Cook the cream mixture at 300°F (150° C) for approximately 1 hour, or until it is firm.

Take out of the oven and let cool. To serve, flip the cream carefully onto the center of a plate. Dust cocoa powder over top and garnish with whipped cream. You can also serve the cream in the dishes, if you like.

Serves 4

# Panna Cotta with Raspberry Coulis

½ cup (125g) **dried cane sugar**

2 tbsp **water**

¼ cup (60ml) **luke warm water**

1 qt (1 L) **natural whipping cream**

1 tsp **natural vanilla extract**

1 tbsp **orange extract** (orange juice concentrate)

2 ½ tbsp **unpasteurized honey**

2 tbsp **agar agar** (natural gelatine thickener)

**Raspberry Coulis:**

1 ½ cups **raspberries**

½ cup **dried cane sugar**

1 tbsp **lemon rind**

1 tbsp **orange rind**

In a small pot, on medium heat, dissolve dried cane sugar in water until it caramelizes and thickens. Pour enough into each soufflé cup to just cover the bottoms. Set aside.

Bring cream, vanilla extract, orange extract and honey to a boil. Dissolve agar agar in luke warm water until it thickens and add to cream mixture. Whisk thoroughly until agar agar mixture is completely combined. Pour into soufflé cups and set aside to let cool. Refrigerate for 4 to 6 hours.

To make the coulis put all ingredients in a small pot and cook at medium heat until dried cane sugar has dissolved. Pour the mixture into a blender and blend all together. Strain thoroughly to remove seeds. Add 1 tablespoon of the raspberry coulis to the center of each plate. With a small paring knife loosen the panna cotta from the soufflé dish and flip onto plates.

Serves 4

*orange*

# Flax Seed Muffins with Preserve

½ **cup (220g) whole flax seeds**

1 ½ **cups (375ml) kefir or buttermilk**

2 **cups whole wheat flour**

½ **cup (220g) flax meal**

½ **cup (220g) firmly packed cane sugar**

1 **tsp aluminum-free baking powder**

2 **tsp baking soda**

¼ **tsp sea salt**

2 **free-range eggs**

¼ **cup (60 ml) almond oil or melted butter**

1 **tsp natural vanilla extract**

2 **large ripe pears, cut in chunks**

¼ **cup (100g) walnuts, chopped**

**Persimmon Preserve:**

4 **firm persimmons** (or peaches or apricots)**, cut in segments**

1 **tbsp butter**

2 **tbsp dried cane sugar** (not necessary if you're using maple syrup instead of brandy)

**Rind of 1 orange, grated**

**Juice of 1 orange, grated**

**Pinch cinnamon**

**Pinch nutmeg**

2 **tbsp brandy or maple syrup**

Soak flax seeds in kefir or buttermilk for 2 hours. Preheat oven to 380° F (190°C).

In a large bowl, mix flour, flax meal, dried cane sugar, baking powder, baking soda and salt. In another bowl, beat eggs and then add almond oil, vanilla and kefir-soaked flax seeds. Combine ingredients of both bowls, add the pear and gently stir until smooth. Fold in walnuts. Fill 16 muffin cups ¾ full, and bake for 20 minutes. Let them sit on a cooling rack for at least 5 minutes before serving.

To make the preserve, heat the butter on medium heat. Add dried sugar cane and the persimmons. Cook at very low heat until persimmons are caramelized (about 4 minutes). Add the rest of the ingredients and cook for 3 to 4 minutes. Serve warm with muffins.

Yields 16 muffins

# Marble Cake

½ cup (125g) **butter**

½ cup (200g) **dried cane sugar powder**

3 **free-range eggs**

⅔ cup (150g) **whole wheat flour, sifted**

1 tsp **baking powder**

2 tbsp **cocoa powder**

⅛ cup (40ml) **natural milk or water**

¼ cup (100g) **walnuts, chopped**

1 tsp **lemon zest**

## Cake Baking Tips

•If the top of your cake is getting too dark before baking is done, put a sheet of parchment paper over top of it.

•Whenever you bake a cake that has baking powder in it, do not open the oven door during the first 45 minutes of baking or the cake may flop.

•Parchment paper is better to use than wax paper, as it is not as greasy and is a more natural paper.

Preheat oven to 470° F (240° C). In a medium bowl whip the butter until creamy. Using a whisk and stirring continuously (not beating but mixing thoroughly), add the dried cane sugar powder, one whole egg and one egg yolk. Mix the baking powder with ¼ of the flour and sift into the batter. Then carefully (still stirring) add the remaining egg and the leftover egg white. Sift the rest of the flour into the bowl and stir. The batter is not firm, but more like the consistency of mashed potatoes or a thick pancake batter.

Take a little more than half the batter and put it in another bowl. This will be the white part of the marble cake. Set it aside.

Dissolve the cocoa powder in the milk and add to the remaining batter. Mix until batter is brown. Add about half of the walnuts and mix them in. Set chocolate batter aside. Add the remaining nuts and lemon zest to the white batter.

Grease a long loaf pan with butter and put parchment paper inside (make sure the paper sticks up past the top of the pan in case the cake rises above the rim). Then grease the inside of the parchment paper. Put half of the white dough in the pan. Then put half of the chocolate dough on top. Put the remaining white batter on top of that and finish with the chocolate batter. With a fork, slightly mix the batter to make swirls of chocolate and white.

Put the pan in the oven and turn heat down to 350° F (180°C). Bake for 1 hour and 15 minutes. The cake is ready when a wooden skewer poked in the center comes out clean when removed. Let the cake cool in the pan for about half an hour and then remove to a cooling rack. Serve warm or cold.

Serves 8

# Figs Stuffed with Chestnut Cream

If you want to impress your guests, or yourself for that matter, this recipe is the perfect way to do it. Simple to make, healthy and fun, this dessert is unique.

**8 ripe black figs**

**½ cup (200g) chestnuts**

**1 free-range egg yolk**

**½ cup (200g) Mascarpone or cream cheese**

**2 tbsp maple syrup**

**½ tsp cardamom powder**

**1 large persimmon** (or an apricot or peach)

Wash figs carefully (do not squeeze). Dry with paper towel and cut the tops off (so they look like little hats). Carefully, with a teaspoon, remove the seeds from inside the figs and set aside. Purée the chestnuts in a blender or food processor. Add the fig seeds, egg yolk, Mascarpone or cream cheese, maple syrup and cardamom and purée until smooth.

Put the mixture in a pastry bag and squeeze the mixture into the figs. Put the figs' "hats" back on top and garnish with a piece of persimmon.

Serves 2

*apricot*

# Three Layer Ice Cream

Good old-fashioned ice cream is a dessert favorite. Making your own ice cream means never having to eat the unnaturally sweet and preservative-laden choices available in the stores.

### Ice Cream:

**1 cup (240ml) natural whipping cream**

**2 free-range egg yolks**

**⅓ cup (120g) dried cane sugar**

**Seeds from 1 vanilla bean** (or 1 tbsp of natural vanilla extract)

**½ cup (120ml) unsweetened melted chocolate,** (if you're making the Chocolate Ice Cream)

In a large bowl, mix all ingredients and transfer to a saucepan. At medium heat stir the mixture with a wooden spoon until it develops a slightly thick consistency. Make sure it doesn't boil. Set aside until completely cooled.

### At this point add:

**½ cup (200g) blackberries to make Blackberry Ice Cream;**

**or ¼ cup (100g) of whole pistachio nuts, shelled, for Vanilla Ice Cream with Pistachio;**

**or ½ cup (125g) of unsweetened chocolate chips for Chocolate Ice Cream.**

Put plastic wrap (with at least a 3" overlap) in the pan. Make each of the ice cream recipes separately. Freeze the first layer for four hours, add the second layer to the first and freeze for four more hours and do the same with the third.

To serve the Three Layer Ice Cream, remove it from the pan by lifting on the plastic wrap. Put it on a serving plate, slice and serve.

Serves 6

# Fruit Trio Sorbet

## Pomegranate:

**1 cup** (250ml)
**Pomegranate juice,
freshly squeezed**

**2 tbsp unpasteurized
honey**

**¼ cup organic pear juice**

**1 free-range egg white**

## Persimmons:

**4 ripe persimmons**
(or apricots)**, peeled
and cut in chunks**

**2 tbsp honey**

**1 tsp lemon juice**

**¼ cup organic
apple juice**

**1 free-range egg white**

## Mango:

**Flesh from 2 ripe mangos**

**2 tbsp honey**

**1 tsp lemon juice**

**¼ cup organic or
freshly squeezed
carrot juice**

**1 free-range egg white**

In a blender blend pomegranate juice with honey and pear juice and freeze for at least 1 hour, or until it is slushy. In a large bowl, whisk egg white until stiff. Mix egg white with semi-frozen pomegranate mixture and combine thoroughly. Freeze until firm. To serve, scoop sorbet balls and put in glasses.

Follow directions above, substituting different fruit and juices. To serve, scoop balls and put in glasses or bowls.

*mango*

Follow directions above, substituting different fruit and juices. To serve, scoop balls and put in glasses or bowls.

### Add some Fizz
If you only want to use one kind of juice, you may replace the second juice with sparkling water.

# Chocolate Mini Cakes

1 cup (440 g) **cocoa powder** (Rapunzel)

1 ½ cups (300g) **dried cane sugar**

**4 free-range eggs**

¼ **cup** (50g) **whole wheat flour**

**1 tsp baking powder**

**2 tbsp natural vanilla extract**

**1 tbsp maple syrup**

¼ **cup** (80 g) **sliced almonds**

**1 tbsp butter**

Grease soufflé dishes (2" width) with the butter. Combine all ingredients (except for almonds) in blender. Blend on medium until you have a runny chocolate sauce. Add almonds (saving some for the top) and pour mixture into dishes. Sprinkle remaining almonds on top. Set the dishes in a lasagna-type pan and carefully pour water around the dishes, until it covers about ⅔ of the height of them. Bake for 35 to 40 minutes at 380°F (190°C). Take the cakes out of the dishes and serve with fruit and natural whipping cream.

Serves 4

# sources

for natural unrefined oils:
**Flora**
7400 Fraser Park Drive
Burnaby BC V5J 5B9
Tel:(604) 436–6000
Tel:1-800-663-0617 (Western Canada)
Tel:1-800-387-7541 (Eastern Canada)

for juicers:
**Teldon of Canada Ltd.**
7432 Fraser Park Drive
Burnaby, BC V5J 5B9
Tel:      (604) 436-0545
Orders:1-800-663-2212
Fax:      (604) 435-4862
E-mail: teldon@ultranet.ca

for Rapadura:
**Rapunzel Pure Organics**
2424 State Route
203 Valatia 12184 USA
Tel: 1-800-207-2814
Tel: (518) 392-8620
Fax:(518) 392-8630
E-mail: mkg@rapunzel.com

First published in 2000 by
**alive books**
7436 Fraser Park Drive
Burnaby BC V5J 5B9
(604) 435–1919
1-800–661–0303

© 2000 by **alive** books

Artwork:
  Liza Novecoski
  Terence Yeung
  Raymond Cheung
Food Styling:
  Fred Edrissi
Photography:
  Edmond Fong (recipe photos)
  Siegfried Gursche
Photo Editing:
  Sabine Edrissi-Bredenbrock
Editing:
  Sandra Tonn

Canadian Cataloguing in
Publication Data

Edrissi, Fred
  Chef's Healthy Desserts

(**alive** natural health guides, 9
ISSN 1490-6503)
ISBN 1-55312-012-4

Printed in Canada

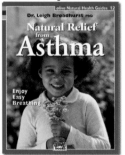